THE DROPPING *of* THE ATOMIC BOMBS

A HISTORY PERSPECTIVES BOOK

Roberta Baxter

Published in the United States of America by Cherry Lake Publishing
Ann Arbor, Michigan
www.cherrylakepublishing.com

Consultants: Peter Kuznick, PhD, Professor of History and Director of the
Nuclear Studies Institute, American University; Marla Conn, ReadAbility, Inc.
Editorial direction: Red Line Editorial
Book design and illustration: Sleeping Bear Press

Photo Credits: Library of Congress, cover (left), cover (middle), cover
(right), 1 (left), 1 (middle), 1 (right), 4, 17, 27; AP Images, 6, 8, 10, 14, 22;
United Nations/Yosuke Yamahata/AP Images, 12; Stanley Troutman/AP
Images, 19, 30; U.S. Marine Signal Corps/AP Images, 24

Library of Congress Cataloging-in-Publication Data

Baxter, Roberta, 1952-
  The dropping of the atomic bombs / Roberta Baxter.
    pages cm. -- (Perspectives library)
  ISBN 978-1-62431-665-4 (hardcover) -- ISBN 978-1-62431-692-0 (pbk.)
-- ISBN 978-1-62431-719-4 (pdf) -- ISBN 978-1-62431-746-0 (hosted
ebook)
 1. Hiroshima-shi (Japan)--History--Bombardment, 1945--Juvenile
literature. 2. Atomic bomb--History--20th century--Juvenile literature. 3.
Manhattan Project (U.S.)--History--Juvenile literature. I. Title.

  D767.25.H6B39 2013
  940.54'2521954--dc23

                        2013029376

Cherry Lake Publishing would like to acknowledge the work of
The Partnership for 21st Century Skills. Please visit www.p21.org
for more information.

Printed in the United States of America
Corporate Graphics Inc.
January 2014

TABLE OF CONTENTS

In this book, you will read about the dropping of the atomic bombs during World War II from three perspectives. Each perspective is based on real things that happened to real people who were involved in or experienced the dropping of the bombs. As you'll see, the same event can look different depending on one's point of view.

Peggy Johnson
Manhattan Project Chemist

In June 1943, I finally found out my husband's secret. Since he earned his PhD in physics the previous summer, Bob had worked for a top-secret project at the University of Chicago. He couldn't tell me anything about his work. I had just received my PhD in chemistry the previous month and had gotten a job working on the Manhattan Project for our government. It was the same project Bob was working on.

On the project, Bob and other scientists had been experimenting with nuclear fission. They had been splitting uranium **atoms** by blasting them with streams of **neutrons**. When the neutrons hit a uranium atom, the atom breaks apart. Large amounts of energy are released. When the uranium atom splits, more neutrons are released, and they hit more atoms. So the process continues in a chain reaction. Scientists were trying to control this type of chain reaction in order to produce enormous amounts of energy.

I began working with a newly discovered **element**, plutonium. Plutonium was first produced in 1941 by bombarding uranium with neutrons in a nuclear reactor. My task as a **chemist** was to do more research on plutonium. The project managers told us that they hoped this would allow us to make atomic bombs that would help us win the war. An atomic

◀ *Scientists on the Manhattan Project controlled the atomic chain reactions needed to set off a bomb.*

bomb will produce tremendous energy by splitting the atoms of uranium and plutonium.

I remember that Sunday afternoon on December 7, 1941. Bob and I were dancing to music from the radio when an announcement cut in on the station. The Japanese had attacked our country's naval base in Pearl Harbor, Hawaii. More than 2,000 U.S. military men were killed. The next day, the United States declared war on Japan, and our country entered World War II. The United States and its **allies** were soon at war not only with Japan, but also with Germany and Italy.

I was so afraid that Bob would have to **enlist** in the army. But as a scientist, he was more valuable working at home on scientific projects geared toward supporting the war effort. Because Bob is a **physicist**, he worked on a different part of our project than I did. Sometimes we talked in the lab, but we could not say anything about our work at home or in the city. A spy from Germany might hear. They were working on the same ideas.

I had been on the project for a couple months when we learned our part of the project was moving from Chicago to New Mexico. The government built a new town on a mesa in the desert for us. It was a very secret town called Los Alamos. Bob and I have been living in Los Alamos for about a year and a half, and life is very different here. Everyone has to carry an identification pass around town, even children. Almost everyone is a scientist of some kind. Military men are here to guard us and the secret town.

THINK ABOUT IT

▶ What is the main point of this paragraph? Pick out one piece of evidence that supports your answer.

No other people can live here. We can't even tell our families where we are now. The army is constantly reminding us to keep the project and even our location secret. Our mail goes to one post-office box and then is brought to us. The military leader of the project is General Leslie R. Groves. He heads the program through the U.S. Army Corps of Engineers.

Here in New Mexico, our head boss is Robert Oppenheimer. We call him Oppy. He is a brilliant physicist, and Bob and I are honored to work with him. Every evening, scientists gather at the Lodge, the best place to eat in our small

◄ *Robert Oppenheimer, left, and General Leslie R. Groves, right, were two heads of the Manhattan Project.*

town. People sit around tables and talk about the Manhattan Project we're working on.

Nothing is called by its real name. Physicists are called "fizzlers" and chemists are known as "stinkers." It's not the best nickname, but we chemists do use lots of smelly chemicals. We call the atomic bomb the "gadget."

Some of the scientists are concerned about making a new bomb for the military to use. We know that if it works, it will kill many people. One hundred and fifty-five of the project's scientists have written a letter to ask the government not to use the bomb. They want to show the power of the bomb but not use it on one of our enemies in the war. They fear the kind of future world they will create if other countries also develop such bombs. Humanity, they

SECOND SOURCE

► Find another source on the Manhattan Project and compare the information there to the information in this source.

know, might not survive. I think of the many thousands who have already died in this war, and I want it to be over. Maybe our bomb will make that happen.

Just this month, in July 1945, several scientists left Los Alamos to travel south to an isolated place in the desert called Trinity Site, about 230 miles from

▲ *Scientists and crew members rig the atomic bomb to be tested at the Trinity Site in July 1945.*

Los Alamos. The gadget was going to be tested there. Several of us gathered at a point 27 miles north of Trinity Site to observe the test. We spread out blankets, drank coffee, and talked quietly. Then just before sunrise, we saw a brilliant light to the south—brighter than the sun. It was as if the atmosphere were on fire. Next we heard a low rumble, like thunder. The gadget worked.

TWO BOMBS

Two types of bombs were made at Los Alamos. One called Little Boy was a uranium bomb. Scientists were confident it would work, so it was not tested. Another nicknamed Fat Man was made of plutonium. It was a more complicated bomb, so the bomb was tested at Trinity Site to make sure it worked. Another bomb was then built after the first was tested.

Haru Tanaka

Hiroshima Witness

It is August 1945, and I am 12 years old. My country has been at war since 1937, so many of my memories are of war. One of our military leaders recently said on the radio that we are winning the war and that it will soon be over.

I am glad for that. The war has been tough for us. On a night in April 1942, bombers flew over Japan's capital city of Tokyo, where my family used to live. They dropped bombs on our city, and a steel mill and a couple of other facilities were destroyed. I guess we had not thought that U.S. bombers could fly far enough to reach Japan. My father worked in the steel mill that was destroyed, but luckily he survived.

Then a few months ago, in March 1945, we heard the drone of many planes. This time they were flying lower than before. Then the **firebombs** started falling. Soon, fires were burning all across Tokyo. One bomb exploded a street away from our house. We managed to run away with only a few things. But our house burned. Thousands of people died from the fires. My parents feared that the firebombs would keep coming. So we moved to the home of my grandmother in Hiroshima, about 500 miles west of Tokyo. My father is too old to join the army, so he has found a factory job near the harbor.

My grandmother lives on the edge of Hiroshima. One of my favorite places to go is a small hill just outside of the city. From the top of my hill, I can see most of the city. I can spot the rivers as they run to the sea and the harbor where many soldiers board their ships.

▲ *A U.S. bomber plane takes off on its way to bomb Tokyo in April 1942.*

The morning of August 6, 1945, was clear and warm. I left my grandmother's house early and climbed up my hill. Soon after I was at the top, I heard the faint drone of a plane. Then the world blew up. From the far side of my hill came a brilliant flash of light. When I turned to see what it was, a blast threw me down on the ground, and I felt a big wave of heat come over me. From my place on the ground, I saw a huge cloud rising into the sky. It was a mix of white, gold, blue, and purple. My stunned brain wondered what it was. How could the Americans have firebombed us here? I didn't hear the hundreds of planes like I had in Tokyo.

When I got up, I saw it. The city was gone. It looked like many nights of firebombing had occurred. Most of what I could see was rubble and flattened buildings.

ANALYZE THIS

▶ Analyze the accounts of Peggy Johnson and Haru Tanaka. How are they different? How are they similar?

Fires were burning everywhere. My mind could not take it in.

I thought about my family, and I ran back to my grandmother's house. A man came walking toward me with skin badly burned and holding out his arms. I was frightened and didn't know what to do, so I just ran.

As I neared my grandmother's house, I saw two of the walls had been torn off in the blast. Debris was scattered around the house. I began calling for my father, mother, sisters, and grandmother. I heard a faint cry and found my baby sister against one of the walls that was still standing, still in her little bed. She seemed to be okay. My mother staggered in from the back of the house. She had burns on her face, but she was not as badly wounded

SECOND SOURCE

▶ Find another source on the bombing of Hiroshima and compare the information there to the information in this source.

▲ *The atomic bomb that was dropped on Hiroshima wiped out most of the city.*

as the person I had seen in the street. Then I realized that she couldn't see. She was blinded from the bomb. I didn't understand how that could happen. I got her to sit down, and I looked for my father, older sister, and grandmother.

I remembered that my father was at work. I refused to think about him. My father had told me before that our enemies would usually try to bomb military sites. So I knew the bombs would have concentrated on the military sites near the harbor, where my father was working.

I found my older sister under a collapsed wall. She had a broken leg and some burns, but I was able to pull her out. Then my grandmother came in, and she had a few burns too. She had been at a neighbor's house. She said the hospitals would be crowded, so she bandaged my sister's leg and my mother's eyes, and she treated all our burns. She found a burn across my back that I didn't even know about.

I don't know how many hours we sat in that damaged house and waited for my father, for help, for anything. Neighbors passed by looking for their families. Many had burned faces and arms. What could have happened? I didn't hear the planes with

▲ *A man walks through the rubble where a house once stood in Hiroshima.*

their loads of firebombs. I explained to my mother what I saw around us. Fortunately, her eyes were getting better. She said she could tell that it was getting dark.

As night fell, all of us huddled on the floor, holding on to each other. But my mind could not rest. I relived that brilliant flash, the blast, and that strange cloud. My name, Haru, means sunlight, but I hope to never again see a brilliant light like the one the bomb gave off.

Two days have passed since the bomb hit us. My grandmother is now dead. She was sick for a while and then she was gone. Father has not come home, and we are coming to realize he may have died in the blast.

One of our neighbors said she heard about the bomb. She said it is a new type of bomb that has never been dropped before. It is more powerful than all the firebombs put together. She also said there is a bomb sickness all over the destroyed city. The new bomb is capable of many things we had never thought possible. And certainly, my country cannot be winning the war when such a terrible bomb as this was dropped on us.

RADIATION

When an atomic bomb explodes, it gives off **radiation**. People exposed to radiation can get sick. They experience nausea, vomiting, vision loss, hair loss, cancer, and sometimes death. Many people in Japan got radiation sickness caused by the atomic bombs. Some of the victims showed no signs of physical injury, and the radiation effects often did not show until weeks after the bombing.

3

Danny Shields

U.S. Secretary of War Staff Member

In 1943, I had the honor of working for Henry Stimson, the U.S. secretary of war. It was a busy time, as we were in the middle of World War II. The United States had entered the war in December 1941. My job was handling papers from Mr. Stimson's office. I typed up memos, made sure they were sent to the right people, took notes during meetings, and filed the papers for safekeeping. Because of my job, I gained an understanding that atomic bombs might be used to try to end the war.

When I started my job, the United States and other **Allied Powers** were fighting the Japanese on Japanese islands in the Pacific Ocean. Each island attack seemed to leave more of our men dead or wounded. The fighting had just started on the large island of New Guinea. That struggle lasted two years. I followed it through reports sent to Mr. Stimson.

One of the island battles that really disturbed me was on Saipan, a tiny island south of Japan. In July 1944, our marines and soldiers invaded Saipan after our navy ships had bombed it. Our **troops** were supposed to capture the island from the Japanese. But the Japanese also had their orders. We learned that they were told to die for their emperor and that each Japanese soldier should kill seven Americans before he died. The fighting was fierce, and nearly 14,000 U.S. troops were killed, wounded, or missing. The Japanese lost approximately 30,000. One tragedy was that many Japanese civilians committed suicide by jumping off a cliff. They had been told that the Americans would torture them. That battle pointed out to me how determined the Japanese were to win this war.

In early 1945, I received a promotion and began to handle the papers of Mr. Stimson directly. That is when I learned of the possibility of a new bomb that

▲ *U.S. troops carried out ground attacks during the invasion of Saipan.*

could end this war. Scientists were working feverishly to build atomic bombs as part of the Manhattan Project. Their military leader, General Groves, sent updates on the project to Mr. Stimson's office, and I organized and filed them in a top-secret cabinet.

When President Franklin Roosevelt died on April 12, 1945, Harry Truman became president. He knew nothing about the atomic bombs until Mr. Stimson told him that night. At a follow-up meeting with President Truman, Mr. Stimson said, "Within four months we shall in all probability have completed the most terrible weapon ever known in human history, one bomb of which could destroy a whole city."

A committee, including an advisory panel of four scientists, was chosen to guide President Truman on the use of an atomic bomb. It was its recommendation that a bomb be used on Japan as soon as possible to end the war. Not everyone agreed. One hundred fifty-five Manhattan Project scientists signed a petition urging the president not to use the atomic bombs. They feared that by using these bombs, the United States would be "opening the door to an era of devastation on an unimaginable scale."

Military officials were also making plans to invade Japan to end the war without the atomic bombs. They estimated that the invasion would start in November 1945 and last for a year. Estimates of the number of casualties this would lead to varied widely.

President Truman later claimed that General George Marshall told him the United States would lose half a million men in an invasion. But most wartime estimates were much lower. Still, it was a horrible plan to think about.

On July 26, the U.S. government sent a message to the Japanese government giving them an

ANALYZE THIS

▶ Analyze the perspectives of Haru Tanaka and Danny Shields. How are they different? How are they similar?

The atomic bombs' explosions made mushroom-shaped clouds high in the sky. ▶

ultimatum. If the country did not surrender, it could expect "prompt and utter destruction." The message did not assure the Japanese that they could keep their emperor, whom most worshipped as a god, or let them know that the powerful Soviet Union was about to join the war against Japan on the Allied side. And it did not mention that the United States had developed atomic bombs, which it was prepared to use. Japanese leaders did not respond to the United States' ultimatum.

President Truman ordered the atomic bombs to be dropped on Japan. On August 6, 1945, a B-29 bomber dropped the first bomb on Hiroshima. Nothing was heard from the Japanese. They did not surrender. Early on the morning of August 9, the Soviet Union invaded Manchuria in northeastern China, as it had promised Presidents Roosevelt and Truman it would. The Japanese had previously invaded Manchuria and were occupying the area. The second atomic bomb was dropped on Nagasaki 11 hours after the Soviet invasion, still on August 9.

DEATHS AT HIROSHIMA AND NAGASAKI

The atomic bomb dropped on Hiroshima destroyed most of the city. It immediately killed 80,000 people. The bomb dropped on Nagasaki immediately killed an estimated 40,000. Tens of thousands more died later due to exposure to radiation. Death tolls in each city almost doubled by the end of 1945 and continued to grow over the following years as victims died from cancer and other diseases.

The atomic bombs produced widespread death and destruction. But they did not convince the Japanese to surrender, because the United States had already been firebombing and destroying Japanese cities. It was the Soviet invasion that convinced Japanese leaders that defeat was inevitable. The Japanese surrendered on August 14.

World War II was over in the Pacific. Our troops realized they would be coming home rather than invading the Japanese islands. This was great news for our country. Yet it came at a huge cost.

THINK ABOUT IT

▶ Determine the main point of this chapter and pick out one piece of evidence that supports your answer.

LOOK, LOOK AGAIN

This image shows Hiroshima after the atomic bomb was dropped. Use this photo to answer the following questions:

1. What would a scientist working on the Manhattan Project think when he or she saw this image?

2. How would a survivor of Hiroshima describe the devastation to a family member in another country?

3. What would an employee of the U.S. Department of War think when he or she saw this picture?

GLOSSARY

Allied Powers (AL-ide POU-urs) in World War II, Great Britain, France, the United States, the Soviet Union, and other countries that were fighting the Axis Powers of Germany, Italy, and Japan

allies (AL-eyes) countries that are on the same side during a war or disagreement

atoms (AT-uhms) the smallest particles of an element that have all the properties of the element

chemist (KEM-ist) a scientist who studies substances, what they are made of, and how they react with each other

element (EL-uh-muhnt) a fundamental substance that is made up of atoms

enlist (en-LIST) to join the military

firebombs (FIRE-bahms) bombs that start fires

neutrons (NOO-trahns) extremely small particles that form the centers of atoms

physicist (FIZ-i-sist) a scientist who studies matter, forces, and energy

radiation (ray-dee-AY-shuhn) atomic particles that are sent out from a radioactive substance, such as uranium

troops (TROOPS) soldiers

ultimatum (uhl-tuh-MAY-tuhm) a final demand that carries the threat of punishment if ignored

LEARN MORE

Further Reading

Elish, Dan. *The Manhattan Project.* New York: Children's Press, 2007.
Lawton, Clive A. *Hiroshima: The Story of the First Atom Bomb.* Cambridge, MA: Candlewick, 2004.
Sheinkin, Steve. *Bomb: The Race to Build and Steal the World's Most Dangerous Weapon.* New York: Roaring Brook, 2012.

Web Sites

Nagasaki Atomic Bomb Museum
http://www.city.nagasaki.lg.jp/peace/english/abm/
This Web site has more information about the Nagasaki bombing, including information about damage to the city and survivors' stories.

Voices of the Manhattan Project
http://www.manhattanprojectvoices.org/
Visitors to this Web site can listen to interviews of many of the people involved in the Manhattan Project.

INDEX

ABOUT THE AUTHOR

Roberta Baxter has visited Trinity Site and Los Alamos. She has a degree in chemistry. Her writing has covered science, history, and biography for students of all ages. Her published work includes more than 15 books and numerous articles.